101 Essays to Empower You to Up Your Game

Frank Agin
Founder & President
AmSpirit Business Connections

ISBN: 978-1-967521-05-0

Published by:
418 Press, A Division of Four Eighteen Enterprises LLC
Post Office Box 30724, Columbus, Ohio 43230-0724

Acknowledgement

In sincere appreciation of Jeff Houck.

You cannot have a second franchisee until you get the first. And you cannot get the first until you find someone with the courage to take a chance. That's you.

Thank you!

Table of Contents

Look For These Other Books in This Series

101 Essays to Empower You to Rise & Thrive
101 Essays to Empower You to Build Momentum
101 Essays to Empower You to Limitless Reach
101 Essays to Empower You to Elevate Your Influence
101 Essays to Empower You to Peak Performance
101 Essays to Empower You to The Winning Edge
101 Essays to Empower You to Live Unstoppable
101 Essays to Empower You to Achieve Greatness
101 Essays to Empower You to Break Barriers

Introduction

This book comes from the insight and creativity of Frank Agin.

Who is Frank? He is the founder and president of AmSpirit Business Connections, an organization that empowers entrepreneurs, sales representatives, and professionals to become successful and gain more referrals through networking.

He is the author of several books, including Foundational *Networking: Building Know, Like and Trust to Create a Lifetime of Extraordinary Success* and *The Three Reasons You Don't Get Referrals*. See all his books and programs at frankagin.com.

Finally, Frank shares information and insights on professional relationships, business networking and best practices for generating referrals on the Networking Rx podcast.

In the summer of 2018, he started planning this short-form podcast. As he mapped out what he wanted to bring to an audience of entrepreneurs, sales representatives, and professionals, he knew he'd have hundreds of programs.

But in addition to all that content, Frank noticed he also had a plethora of other materials—instructive, insightful, and inspirational. All this additional content was worthwhile, but none of it was long enough to create a full episode of Networking Rx.

Not wanting the material to go to waste, Frank developed it into short essays—approximately 150 words each. Then he started to record and share those segments daily under the brand Networking Rx Minutes.

For years, he shared a daily message of empowerment, intuition, and hope. This is a compilation of 100 of those essays. Enjoy.

-1-
Innovating Your Success

Since the dawn of time, as humans, we've been looking for ways to make life easier. We have gone (in a mere tick of the geological clock) from carving messages on cave walls to sending texts at lightning speed from one corner of the world to the other. We once walked everywhere … we now walk nowhere.

We are not lazy. We are innovative. This serves to make us (and hopefully keep us) the dominate species on the planet. As humans we're always on the lookout for easier ways to do things.

When it comes to achieving success, heed the game plan put forth by your ancestors. Innovate. Harness technology. Pay attention to what others are doing. And then figure out how to do it with a little less effort.

Yes, success requires hard work. But it takes smart work too.

-2-
The Power of Reconnecting

When you think of networking, you likely conjure up images of meeting new people. Although meeting new people is an important part of developing your network, you can also develop your network by cultivating relationships with people you already know.

Think about it. If you are between the ages of 19 and 90, you already know more people than you will meet over the next year, maybe two. Therefore, to maximize your networking effort, focus on reconnecting with those you already know rather than devoting lots of attention to meeting new people.

Remember, networking is about getting people to know, like and trust you. So, the advantage of reconnecting with people with whom you have a history is that these people presumably already "like and trust" you. And regardless of your aspirations, that gets you a bunch closer a whole lot sooner.

-3-
Location, Location, Location

In fishing, you go to where the fish are or will be, right? To do anything otherwise makes absolutely no sense.

Well, the same logic holds true in networking. At events, appropriately position yourself.

If you stand outside the mainstream of human flow (or worse, sit off to the side), you virtually eliminate your opportunity for having anything come from the networking event – immediately or ever. You've basically dropped your line and bait into water where there are no fish. It makes no sense, right?

The best strategy is to stand where you will most likely encounter people. Position yourself near the entrance. Locate yourself in close proximity to the food or coffee. Stake out real estate close to other high-traffic areas.

In any of these spots, you will encounter people. Like a parade, they will meander by for you to meet.

-4-
The Octuple Co-Championship

In 2008, the Marquette Redmen and Orchard Lake St. Mary Eagles faced-off for an epic Michigan high school hockey state championship game.

These two teams came into the game with similar records. These two teams each had aspirations of winning a state title. These two teams were equally matched.

In fact, these teams were so equally matched that the state championship went beyond regulation time and into overtime. And then beyond the first overtime to a second. Then on to a third ... then a fourth ... a fifth, sixth, seventh and on into an eighth overtime.

Finally, after the eighth overtime, officials suspended the game, declaring these two teams as co-champions.

No doubt you have goals and aspirations. No doubt there are others who want the same things too. Don't get distracted. Focus less on being number one and just direct your energies on being great.

-5-
Advice From Thomas Jefferson

Thomas Jefferson once said, "Nothing gives one person so much advantage over another as to remain always cool and unruffled under all circumstances."

Jefferson was right. You see, when you allow people to get under your skin or situations to distract you, you expend a tremendous amount of energy just to gain back some power you never should have lost.

You worry about how it might taint people's impression of you. And you lose focus on the aspects of your life that drive you towards success. From there
you become a version of yourself that is far less than ideal.

Yes, you will encounter people who attempt to distract you from your vision of success and the efforts to get you there. And, no, you cannot control the conditions that surround you. But you can always choose to respond in a cool and unruffled Jeffersonian manner.

-6-
Laugh Yourself to a Better Network

Having a good sense of humor – whether you are creating the laughter or simply enjoying it – is essential to getting people to know, like and trust you.

Ask yourself, who are you drawn to? Someone who expresses his or her sense of humor on an occasional basis or the person who makes every moment ultra-serious?

If you consider this question, even for a moment, you would probably conclude that you would be much more comfortable associating with the person with a sense of humor.

So, enhance your personal brand and draw people to you by embracing humor. You don't necessarily need to be a constant source of levity. You can also add to the lightness of the moment by chuckling at the humor of others.

Go ahead and laugh. It's good for business.

-7-
What to Give?

An almost absolute rule of building relationships is that you need to contribute to the lives of others. This, often, then begs the question, "What should I give?"

What you give to your network can include business referrals, your own business and even a traditional gift. Introductions to others are also of great value. And, of course, information can be priceless, even if it might seem useless to you.

Equally valuable is your time. Listening. Being consultative. Or just offering your encouragement. These gestures are remembered long after the gift card is spent or that funky tie is no longer cute.

As we are reminded each and every holiday season, it's not the gift. It's the thought that counts. This holds true in the professional networking environment, as well. It's not what you give that's important. It's the spirit that moves you.

-8-
Go Ahead and Jump In

Venturing into any networking setting can seem like taking that first summer swim in the nearby lake, pool, or pond. At first, the environment may seem cold and uncomfortable.

As a result, you might come up with ways to avoid going. Like keeping busy at work, trolling social media or relaxing at home while binge-watching your new favorite show. Whatever.

Despite all this, you know it's in your best interest to go. In the past, you've made important contacts. Sometimes got some business. And you always shared a friendly chat, laugh or smile.

Yes, networking can seem like that first summer swim. In the beginning, it's uncomfortable but once you get in, things quickly warm up.
So, when the next event comes along, grab some business cards, drive on over and jump right in. Once you do, after a moment, it feels great.

-9-
The Power of Compliments

While the people around you might all be unique, in some respects they're all the same. One commonality is that they all long to be accepted, recognized, and valued. They all want to know that somehow, in some way they measure up.

And do you know what? You can give anyone a small piece of that at any point. How? Simple. Just offer up a compliment.

It's true. An authentic compliment about how someone looks, what they might have accomplished, or even how they've conducted themselves serves to affirm the value they offer the world.

Moreover, these compliments build rapport and help to enhance your relationship with them, which then benefits you.

So, here's your challenge for today. Find someone. It doesn't matter who. Just find someone and take a moment to fire out a compliment. By the way, you're an awesome person!

-10-
Ignite "Small Talk"

Small talk is important to building any relationship. Small talk, however, is not about you talking. It's about getting the other person talking. This begs the question: What are good questions to get someone talking?

There is no magic. Planning, however, is paramount. So, have a small handful of questions ready to go. A few of these questions could include.

What do you do? How long have you been doing it? How did you become interested in that?

What are some of the projects or assignments you are currently working on?

Outside of work, what occupies you? How did you become interested in that?

These will give you a start. From there, you might want to formulate a series of follow up questions. Again, there is no magic. It is simply a matter of planning how you will get and keep them talking.

-11-
The Formula of Success

While humans have been able to innovate, shape and adapt to the world around them, the general process of success is the same as it always has been.

And there's no short cut to achieving success. The formula of success is made up of universal elements and these universal elements are what we refer to as habits.

The universal habits of success fall into three basic categories.

One, habits of thought or your general attitudes towards yourself, others, and the circumstances around you.

Two, habits of action or your propensity to take steps to accomplish things.

And three, habits of persistence or your willingness to forge ahead even though things might not be going your way.

These three habits make up the formula of success. And the extent to which you consistently and appropriately execute each of these determines your likelihood of success.

-12-
Get Involved

If you're looking for a way to establish yourself, whether at work or in your community, a sure-fire, can't miss, super effective way of doing so is getting involved.

No doubt, wherever you work or wherever you live, there are opportunities to do a little something extra outside your normal day. There are boards, committees, and initiatives on which you can serve.

Any of these activities is a great investment of time. Why? You see, from this service, people will get to know you better, which will surely lead to them liking and trusting you. From this, any number of likely benefits will follow.

Mostly, this effort will serve to establish you in the hearts of others, firmly putting you on their radar. And with that, you'll be on their minds, even if you happen to not be around.

-13-
Still the Best Policy

In 2005, Adam Van Houten, a sophomore at Mt. Gilead High School, was competing in the Ohio High School Division II State Golf Tournament.

At the end of the tournament, Adam had blown away his competition, beating them by seven strokes. He proudly stood in the clubhouse waiting to be anointed as state champion.

As he stood there, however, Adam realized that he had made a mistake on his official score. In fact, he'd only won by six strokes. Though, no one else knew, he felt compelled to own up to his mistake.

And that's what Adam did, knowing that by rule he'd be automatically disqualified from the competition and the state title would be lost. In the wake of his morality, however, he became iconic and was celebrated both in his community and across the state.

The lesson. Winning produces champions. Honesty, however, creates heroes.

-14-
Avoid Rejection

In the book *Power Networking,* authors Donna Fisher and Sandy Vilas share an approach to your networking interactions that virtually eliminates the risk of you being rejected. In the book they say:

> "Rejection is an issue only if your focus is on having someone respond in a particular way. If you are relaying information primarily as a way to mutually share resources, then any response you get will support the flow of the [networking] process."

So, if you approach people with the attitude that you are merely someone who is interested in learning about them or sharing information with them or helping them (independent of what you sell), it's almost impossible for them to reject you. Why would they, right?

Think about it. You cannot help but like someone who is interested in you or sincerely interested in helping you. So become that person.

Frank Agin

-15-
Queens & Worker Bees

Bee hives have a queen and many worker bees. Each is vital in their own way to the lasting success of the hive.

The queen is the visionary, charting a strategy and formulating a plan. And the worker bees put forth the effort to see the vision through. Without the queen, the workers toil aimlessly. Without workers, the queen's vision has no chance.

For you to be successful, you need to operate in a similar manner. You need to act like the queen. Have a vision. And formulate strategies and plans. But at the same time, you need to operate like the workers, being diligent enough to see the vision through.

If you don't have that compelling vision, you'll end up toiling without purpose. But if you aren't committed to working hard, even the greatest vision is pointless. But with both vision and hard work, your life will, well, buzz.

-16-
Singles Score Runs Too!

According to Major League Baseball, far more runs are generated from singles than home runs. Therefore, no team relies entirely on the home run bat day in and day out. Rather, to create success they focus on a strategy involving singles, doubles, and even walks.

You should follow a similar strategy in your approach to developing a network.

Certainly, some contacts will generate immediate results, like clients, jobs, and other opportunities. These are the home runs. So, rejoice at and celebrate these.

Much of your network, however, will piece together with contacts that generate no immediate results or little apparent value at all. Nevertheless, value still exists.

There is opportunity in every contact. While not every contact creates results in and of itself, every contact serves as something upon which you can build. And as these relationships build, it moves you closer to scoring.

-17-
Connect with New People

Don't ever lose sight of the fact that you already have a tremendous network. As such, the lion's share of your time and energy should be devoted to cultivating relationships with those you already know, like and trust.

That said, your network is not static. People in it fall out for all sorts of reasons. Some move. Some retire. Sadly, some pass away. So, left alone, your network will naturally suffer attrition.

With that, it's important that you get out from time to time to create new relationships. Attend networking events. Spend time at trade shows and expos. Volunteer in the community. Socialize when you can.

While not every situation will yield great new contacts, some certainly will. Those alone will be worth all the effort. Because somewhere amongst the litany of people you'll meet is someone with incredible potential for you.

-18-
It's What You Become

One of the many great sayings of Tony Robbins, renowned author, and self-empowerment guru, is "It's not what you get, it's what you become."

Yes, life can throw situations, challenges, and opportunities at you. These things, both good and bad, can test your patience, stretch you, and open doors. In these moments, it's only natural to wonder about or even seek something, such as recognition, compensation, or an enhanced title.

While there might be an argument that you're due some or all of these things, before you get too consumed with "getting yours", take a moment to reflect. What did the experience, good or bad, do for you? Might it have improved your abilities? Might it have shaped your perspective? Might it have enhanced your personal brand? These might be the true benefits of what life has tossed at you.

Remember, it's not what you get, it's what you become.

-19-
Improving Small Talk

Small talk is important. And whether you're decent at it or struggle, know that it's a skill and like any skill you can improve on it. Here are three ideas for doing that.

First, whenever you have idle time, envision having a "small talk" conversation. See yourself asking questions, listening, and sharing.

Second, listen to others who are engaged in small talk, especially those who are good at it. See how they weave from one question to the next and gracefully exit conversations.

Finally, take every opportunity to engage in "small talk." With co-workers. On the phone with vendors. With clients at your next appointment. You will find the more you engage in small talk, the better you get at it.

Remember, working to become more proficient with small talk is a great investment of time, as it serves to build relationships.

-20-
Tend to the Network

When you cook with a crock-pot, you add the ingredients, stir, and season. Then you wait. And wait – occasionally peeking in to stir your concoction. You cannot rush it. In fact, patience is sort of a main ingredient. Nevertheless, in time, the crock-pot will yield something wonderful for you to feast on.

Your networking is much like a crock-pot. You interact with others – give referrals, share information, make introductions, and provide encouragement. Then, you wait. While you wait, however, you continue to interact.

What you hope for may not be immediate. It seldom is. Again, patience is a main ingredient. You cannot rush the process, but you know something wonderful is coming. In time, networking yields wonderful things for you. It essentially gives back what you put in it. Referrals. Contacts. Information. Encouragement.

Like a crock-pot, it pays to tend to your network.

-21-
Habits of Thought

Your attitudes towards yourself, others, and the circumstances around you are really nothing more than habits. After all, while you cannot control the economy, what happens around you or how others treat you, you can have complete control over what goes on in your mind.

Attitudes are habits. Habits of Thought. This explains why two people can feel completely different about the same situation.

One person gets a speeding ticket and seethes inside towards the police, thinking "Seriously. Aren't there more pressing matters for these neo-Nazi patrolmen to pursue?"

While another person under the same circumstances feels an appreciation towards the officer, thinking "I'm not happy about the ticket, but this is a wake-up call for me to slow down so nothing worse comes from my haste."

So, work to build your attitude, by controlling how you react to things both good and bad.

-22-
Unsolicited Generosity

No doubt, when people ask you for assistance and you come through, they're very appreciative. Whether you're giving them a referral, introducing them to a new contact, or providing them valuable information, in that moment, you're the hero. And rightly so!

Do you know what would make you even more of a hero than coming through when they asked? How about you "coming through" without them having to ask at all.

Certainly, however and whenever you give your network a referral, provide someone with valuable information, or connect another to a key contact, it is an extraordinary act of generosity. Imagine if you did it for them without any sort of prompting.

Wow! They'd be totally floored, wouldn't they? You'd create an incredible moment, wouldn't you? It would be something they'd likely remember, wouldn't it? Chances are it'd inspire them to do something for you, right?

So, from time to time, do for others without being asked.

-23-
Mining Networking Events

Networking events are generally not opportunities for closing business. So, you likely won't get clients as a result of them. But if you do, know that this is the exception rather than the rule.

However, the rule for networking events "is" they are for making meaningful connections with others. That said, at events don't consume yourself with meeting as many people as you can. Meaningfully connecting is about quality relationships and not a large quantity of contacts.

So, you are much better off focusing on really connecting with a small handful of people rather than simply collecting dozens of business cards.

Listen, networking events are everywhere. Business after-hours. Tradeshows. Open houses. Socials. Really any gathering of people. Use any or all of these to network.

But as you do, remember to focus on making meaningful connections and building relationships.

-24-
Do You Believe in Miracles?

In 1980, the United States sent a young, relatively inexperienced hockey team to the Winter Olympic Games in Lake Placid, New York. To win the gold medal, the Americans had to defeat the Soviet Union, a team who had recently beat a team of NHL All-Stars.

Despite the epic challenge, the American upstarts prevailed 4-to-3, shocking the Soviet juggernaut. This game will forever be known as the "Miracle On Ice."

This, however, was no miracle. You see, despite being inexperienced, the American team had a clear and compelling vision of what it wanted to achieve. Additionally, they worked hard leading up to and during the Olympics. And, finally, they exhibited incredible determination throughout.

In business and life, there are no miracles either. Rather, you'll drive your success with a powerful vision, hard work, and unfaltering determination to achieve.

-25-
As You Climb, Lift

Mountain climbing is a team effort. Certainly, it requires incredible individual effort to grasp, push and pull oneself to new heights.

But climbers don't go it alone. Rather they coordinate with another. Then, the climbers take turns either supporting, pulling, or pushing others or accepting help in return. To be successful, climbers know they need to help others as they climb, as from that will come help in return.

Mountain climbing is a wonderful metaphor for achieving success. You must grasp for opportunities. You must pull yourself forward. You must push through tough times.

But you're not in life alone. There are others trying to achieve success too. Assist them. Help them grasp opportunities. Pull them along. Push them when they need it most. Why? Because you'll need help too.

Remember, as you climb, you should be lifting.

-26-
Do Your Job

There's a saying in parenthood: "It's not your job to get your kids to love you; it's simply your job to love your kids no matter what."

There is much truth to this. If you're a parent, you know all too well that all you can do is your best. And sometimes that best includes drawing a hard line and making unpopular decisions. That's love in one of its many forms. And you can't control the reaction of a "terrible two," a rebellious teen or any age in between. Just do your job and love your kids.

This adage, however, has broader applications. You can't control what others think about you or how they react to you. All you can control is that you try to do the right things, say the right things, and find ways to like other people. Quite simply, that's your job.

-27-
The Power of Flocking

Titmice are birds that are similar in size, physical characteristics, and intelligence to robins. However, titmice, as a population, seem to learn and adapt at a much faster rate than robins. Why is this?

You see, robins are individualistic, self-serving, and territorial birds. Rather than cooperate, they chase each other off when another robin approaches.

Titmice, on the other hand, are communal birds, relying heavily on other titmice for survival. Through this mutual dependency, they cooperate and collaborate, quickly learning from each other and adapt accordingly.

In short, the titmice gain knowledge from one another. Robins, however, are self-serving and unwilling to share information.

The lesson is that when you interact with others, you learn - new information, new techniques, and new ways of helping others.

So, if you're interested in being more successful, focus on building a network like the titmice, and not the robins.

-28-
Consciously Networking

Do you know someone with a great network? They have an amazing legion of people around them. People who refer them opportunities. People who feed them useful information. People who connect them to other great people.

Do you know someone like this? You likely do and it can leave you envious.

Here's the thing, however: You too can have a strong, productive network. One that's full of opportunities, information and great new contacts.

You can have one. You just cannot do it overnight, or in a week, a month, or a year. It is a process.

Chances are that person who's got that desirable network has been building it for a long time, consistently doing the right things day after day, week after week.

So, don't be discouraged. Know you can do it too. Just set about consciously networking at any opportunity you get.

-29-
Have a Consistent Demeanor

Let's face it, things don't always work out. In fact, sometimes things go horribly wrong. You don't meet your goals. You lose a great client. One of your key employees turns into a threatening competitor. Or any of several dozen other things.

And while these things can and do happen, often they're completely out of your control. Despite the situation or circumstances, however, there is one thing that remains in your control: How you respond.

Know this, people want to associate with those who have a consistent demeanor. They're simply less likely to trust the person whose reactions and moods fluctuate from high to low with the passing events of the day or week.

In summary, people want to associate with someone who's a "good sport" whether or not things are going well. So be one.

-30-
Pre-Networking Networking

In his book, *The Fine Art of Networking*, Andrew Chiodo shares some insight to help you network "before" you arrive at the next event. He says,

[QUOTE] Email three people you want to meet in advance, saying "Hey, I haven't had a chance to meet you and I thought you might be interested in attending the Business First Breakfast. I would really like to meet you there and get acquainted. I want to learn more about you and your business. Let me know if you plan to attend, and we can arrange to talk more then. [UNQUOTE]

This is sage advice from Chiodo. What he suggests not only allows to you to walk into an event with a connection who's looking for you, but it also ensures that the event will be productive.

So, eye your calendar for that next event then reach out to invite someone to meet you there.

-31-
Building Confidence

Are you confident? That is, do you believe that you can achieve what you set out to do? This is confidence. If you have it, you are pointed in the right direction.

If, however, this is not the case, one thing you can do to improve your sense of self-assurance is break your big goals into small, manageable goals.

Afterall, if you accomplish the goals you set for each day, chances are you will meet your weekly goals. Then those weekly goals will ensure that you topple the monthly ones. And then hitting your monthlies three times, will ensure you make your quarter. And if you make your quarters, you'll make your year.

With bite-sized goals, progress is small and steady. But consistently achieving small, daily milestones will build your confidence moment by moment. **And it's that confidence that will propel you to big success.**

-32-
Business Card Distribution

Remember that whenever you meet someone new, chances are you're not the only person they've recently met. This is especially true when you're out and about networking at events.

Therefore, be sure to always have business cards with you. These little "leave behinds" serve as a big reminder as to who you are and who you're associated with.

But more than ensuring that you have business cards, you should endeavor to make sure that the ones you have are clean and crisp. After all, giving away one that is bent, smudged or damaged is almost worse than not giving away one at all.

Also, if you make a point of giving someone your card, why not give them a couple. This enables them to either forward your business card onto someone else or keep your card in multiple locations.

-33-
Do Something for Others

The most effective way to endear yourself to others is by adding value to them. Alternately stated, when you help others somehow you endear yourself to them.

This then leaves you asking the question, "What can I do to help others?"

Here is a simple means of getting at the answer to this question without ever having to ask them. Simply ask yourself this: "In general terms, what are things that others can do for me?"

You should have no problem coming up with a litany of items.

With that list, take the initiative and do similar things for others. You'd like comments on your social media articles, right? So would they. You'd like to meet successful people in related fields. Them too. Get the idea?

There is no mystery. Others need what you need. Knowing this, it's a simple matter of taking action.

-34-
Star-Spangled Seamstress

Ask any school kid who made the first America flag, and you'll gleefully get the answer: Betsy Ross!

From time to time, we might not be able to name the current president, but we all know that George Washington asked Betsy to sew the original Stars and Stripes. But what you might not know is that networking played a role.

You see, Washington had long been familiar with Ross' husband as their families interacted each Sunday sitting in adjacent pews at Church.

So, when Washington needed the services of someone who knew their around a needle and thread, he didn't have to go far.

The point is that networking is nothing new. It helped form this country. It built it into a great nation. If you let it, networking will build your life.

No, networking is nothing new. But it is, well, revolutionary.

-35-
The Universal Language

Laughter, which is the productive result of humor, is the universal language. It is present in every culture. It is the one quality that you have in common with everyone on the planet. Young. Old. Rich. Poor. Everyone.

Laughter and humor remind others that you are human. It is something with which anyone can identify, and it is something to which everyone is drawn.

In short, humor helps you build know, like and trust. It is nearly impossible to dislike someone who has made us laugh or is genuinely laughing at something funny.

As such, all things being equal, you would opt to associate with the individual who demonstrates a good sense of humor over someone who does not. Thus, humor is important to building relationships as well as your personal brand.

So, while you should be smart about it, endeavor make someone laugh today!

-36-
Enlist Connectors

Let's face it: You can always use one more "great" connection.

Meeting a "great" new contact, however, is not always easy, right? After all, high quality contacts can tend to be overrun with lots of other people looking to get on their radar. And you reaching out to them might make you feel like you're just part of that clamor. As such, you might become hesitant to contact "that" person.

Rather than hesitate, however, consider asking another person to act as a go-between for you. After all, chances are, anyone you're looking to meet is connected to someone you already know.

And here's the thing, most any decent person in your network will gladly step up and do this for you. Plus, and here's the really neat part, they'll be flattered that you asked.

So, grow your network of great people by working through the great people you already know.

-37-
The Responsibility of Leadership

Management books, seminars and business gurus will advise you to set about prioritizing tasks and then delegating anything that's not imperative for you to do. Makes sense, right?

This implies that you should push routine and administrative tasks to underlings or outsourced resources. In short, work smarter and you'll end up doing less.

Management is not leadership, however. As a leader, while you might have removed from your plate certain mundane things, you need to fill it back up (and then some) with activities that serve those around you.

No, you may no longer be making copies or scheduling meetings, but you need to devote time and attention to developing the abilities of others, empowering their well-being, and ensuring your entire network is high functioning.

Remember, leadership is not a license to do less; leadership is a responsibility to do more.

-38-
Your Own Sales Force

Wouldn't it be great to have a sales force for your business? You know, a small army of quality men and women looking to open doors for you.

Well, you do. Around you are legions of people who could effectively serve as your sales force. It's your network. These are people you're likely helping and so it's only natural they'd want to help you in return.

Essentially, you are the sales manager to your network and your task, over time is to do three things:

One, educate them on how to recognize opportunities for you;

Two, empower them on how to generally talk about your industry or profession; and,

Three, coach them on how to work you into the conversation.

These things take some work and forethought. But if you do it right, you'll have created a great sales force, which will be an important asset for you.

-39-
Small Talk to Big Business

"Small talk" is a great warm-up to real business conversation. At some point, though, there is generally a natural lull when small talk has run its course.

To transition away from "small talk" you can use something like, "Well, all that travel is likely not cheap; what do you do to pay for it?"

This is not a green light to pitch your wares. And don't steer or bait them in that direction. It's merely a way to ease into a more professional discussion of business – yours or theirs.

Keep the tone light. Learn about them; share about yourself. If you do this right, you will have lots of opportunity to gather future business intelligence, pitch them, and close the sale. Remember, people do business with those they know, like and trust. So, you're best to create that environment.

-40-
Unstoppable

In 2008, after severally being injured in battle while deployed in Iraq, doctors told Phil Packer he would never walk again. Despite this, he competed in and finished the 2009 London Marathon on crutches — after rowing the English Channel earlier in the year.

At five years old, Dustin Carter contracted a rare blood disease that claimed both his legs and much of his arms. Nevertheless, in 2008, he finished the high school wrestling season with a 41-2 record.

What limits do you think you have? We all come with different shapes, sizes, and all sorts of abilities. Certainly, some are more able-bodied at certain things than others. That said, you have no real restrictions in life. The only limitations you have are the ones you impose upon yourself. With whatever you want to do, believe that you can and work to make it happen.

You are unstoppable.

-41-
Be Optimistic

Is your glass usually half full? That is, do you tend to look on the more favorable side of events or conditions?

No, life is not perfect. Everyone's life has its share of challenges. And yours is no different. But do you view these challenges as forces conspiring against you? Or do you look into these challenges for the potential opportunity and promise? What do you see?

This is the reality: People may sympathize with a mope, but they do not want to associate with that person long term. Rather, if you are optimistic, people will stand with you and want to partake in whatever you see, even if they do not see it themselves.

Successful people are optimistic and want to associate with the same. And, given a choice, you want to be part of this. Right? So, join the "in" crowd. Be optimistic.

-42-
Outside Your Tribe

Let's dial back time 10,000 years or so. The human existence was very different. We lived in pockets of small tribes that were so spread out that people from other tribes seldom interacted.

So back in that time, if you encountered a strange face, there was a real possibility that it represented a significant threat. Now, fast forward to the 21st century. As humans we still carry with us the apprehension associated with meeting someone new. It's perfectly natural.

This feeling is deep-seated, held over from a very primitive time. And likely felt by everyone. Nevertheless, we need to get a grip on our feelings and remember that civilization has come so far.

Striking up conversations with someone from outside your so-called tribe is no longer a threat, but rather represents opportunities. Great new contacts. Reliable vendors. A treasure trove of useful information.

So, be brave. Step outside of your tribe.

-43-
The Good Wolf

There is an old Cherokee parable that goes something like this:

A fight is going on inside you. It is a terrible fight and it is between two wolves. One is evil - he is anger, envy, sorrow, regret, greed, arrogance, self-pity, guilt, resentment, inferiority, lies, false pride, superiority, and ego. The other is good - full of joy, peace, love, hope, serenity, humility, kindness, benevolence, empathy, generosity, trust, truth, compassion, and faith.

Which wolf will win? The answer: The one you feed.

The lesson is simple: Be sure to fill your mind with positive, uplifting thoughts and at the same time push opposing ones out. Read and listen to materials that helps you lead a kind and compassionate life. Surround yourself with people who are driven by hope, love, and peace.

Do all you can to help the good wolf win.

-44-
Resolving Conflict

You live in a great world, in a great time. The wonder of the Internet has put you literally within seconds and a few keystrokes from the world's accumulated knowledge.

Moreover, the Internet has given birth to the likes of LinkedIn, Facebook, Instagram and other social media. In these, you can feel like you're always somewhat in touch, even with people you haven't seen in years.

And, whether by text or e–mail, you can be in constant communiqué with those who matter most ... worldwide ... 24/7. Understand, however, these should have limitations.

For example, don't rely on text or e-mail as a means to resolve personal conflicts. As the name indicates, "personal" conflicts require "personal" attention and, wonderous as it is, the internet can be impersonal. In these moments, be as human as you can. Pick up the phone at a minimum. Better yet, get face to face if you're able.

-45-
The Importance of Being Engaging

Imagine you walk into a business gathering filled with strangers. Who do you tend to gravitate towards - the person who ignores you or the person who takes the time to make eye contact and say hello?

Now, imagine you are in a meeting with individuals you have met before, but none of whom are extremely familiar with you. With whom do you feel most comfortable engaging in conversation - the person who addresses you by name or the person who obviously does not remember it?

Finally, imagine you are at a social gathering through work. Who do you feel the greatest affinity towards - the person whose conversation with you is limited to business matters or the person who engages you in matters of mutual personal interest?

Do you get the idea? You want to engage with those who engage you. So, endeavor to be the person you want to network with.

-46-
A Lesson from Mulberry Street

While you might have never heard of Theodore Geisel, you've likely heard him referred to by his pseudonym – Dr. Seuss.

In the summer of 1936, Seuss completed his first book titled, *And To Think That I Saw It On Mulberry Street*. Then over the next couple years he got rejected 27 times by publishers, each telling him that his work had no merit.

Upon receiving word of his 27th rejection, Seuss headed home to stage a ceremonial burning of the now tattered manuscript. As he grimly walked along Madison Avenue he met up with an old friend from college, who hours earlier had become juvenile editor of Vanguard Press. Thirty minutes later Vanguard committed to publish Seuss' work, launching his career.

The lesson: There is enormous power in reconnecting with those you already know. Today, reach out to an old contact and see where it takes you.

-47-
The Price of Trusting

If you want to be trusted, you're best to trust others first.

Of course, this doesn't advocate that you take insensible or needless risks. Give to others and trust those deeds will come back to you. Share your hopes, dreams and aspirations and trust that others will do the same. Connect people to others and trust they will connect you within their network too.

Of course, there is a risk of trusting. You risk whatever you put out there not being reciprocated. You risk your time for nothing in return. You even risk feeling foolish. And it's likely that a time or two one or more of these things will happen.

But isn't it a small risk considering all you have to gain?

Yes, being cheated and duped occasionally is the price of trusting. But compare that to the price of continually being suspicious. The price of this apprehension is missing opportunity. Think about it. Trusting others is your best bet.

-48-
Sometimes You Have to Create

After World War II, the United States could no longer tolerate the longstanding mood of deep-seated social segregation. As such, change began, and African Americans were hopeful for a better country ... an equal America.

Although the Civil Rights movement had won some victories relative to education and employment, African Americans still did not have the same rights and opportunities relative to equal housing. So, with representation in government lagging on these issues, on July 29, 1947, a coalition for change met in Tampa, Florida to create the National Association of Real Estate Brokers.

This sparked a movement of people, known as Realtists, dedicated to fair housing for all. A movement that has gone on to win victory after victory in support of its creed of "Democracy In Housing."

The point is this. You can always hope for something, but sometimes you have to create that which you want to be part of.

-49-
Happy Birthday to Someone

Do you know what today is? It's somebody's birthday. It is! The actual age doesn't matter. That's just a number. All that matters, is that it's their birthday … their special day.

Here's the thing. Everyone you know has a birthday. That's the one thing that every living soul on the planet has in common. It might not be today, but at one point this year they have a day on the calendar that's theirs.

It's not religious. It's not the product of a political agenda. It's just their day. It's the day they entered the world, surrounded by love, hope and promise.

Take the time to know and remember the birthdays of the people in your life. You don't need to make a production out of celebrating. But it is a wonderful gesture to simply acknowledge them on their special day.

-50-
Bringing Value

You've achieved nothing alone, so you need others to help you see things through. Right?

However, seeking help from others can seem intimidating. You may feel as if you're interrupting their world to benefit yours.

If you are hesitating to ask of others for this reason, here's a thought. Rather than make it all about you, stop and consider what value you can bring to them.

Yes, you might need "X" from a contact, but you have other contacts to share, information to impart, and potential opportunities to unveil. So, if you're genuinely interested in adding value to others, you should have no reluctance asking for what you need in return.

Knowing that, gather your thoughts, reach out for assistance, and offer what you can in return. While not every situation will work out, some certainly will – those alone will be worth all the effort.

-51-
Own Your Life

You do nothing alone. You've achieved nothing alone. Every accomplishment has somehow involved other people. Think about it.

While that's true, what's also true is that in the end, success is up to you.

Yes, to achieve success you need to involve other people. But if these people don't come through, any potential shortcoming is still on you. In short, you cannot use others as an excuse.

Sure, it was others who gave you contacts, information, opportunities, advice and a whole lot more. But whether or not those things manifested themselves into success as you term it, is on you.

Remember, what others provide are mere steppingstones. You and you alone are responsible for which stones you use and how you step on them.

These are the actions you choose, so you must accept the consequences as well. After all, it's your life. Take ownership of it.

-52-
Returning to Small Talk

Great conversations start with small talk. It warms up the mood, right? Then at some point the dialogue shifts to business – a non-salesy exchange of general information.

However, after the professional conversation has run its course, before the conversation ends, it's important to touch back on something related to your "small talk" conversation.

For example, "Great talking with you. Assuming, you don't get laid up in the hospital skiing between now and then, I would enjoy continuing our conversation over a cup of coffee sometime."

Why is this important? Simple. By returning to "small talk" in this way, you have demonstrated that you were listening and that you remembered.

More subtly, however, you are reflecting back to a part of the conversation when they delighted in your interest in them. And that can do nothing but help endear them to you.

-53-
Stuff Happens

For sure, life can have it share of obstacles and setbacks. You might lose a job. That star employee is now a competitor. That great client might decide to go another direction. What you hope is the love of your life, might not feel the same.

Before you chalk these challenges up to "oh well, that's life," stop to consider the real possibility that these obstacles and setbacks are really not bad things at all.

Maybe, just maybe they're really steppingstones to something better. Perhaps, just perhaps they're a foothold to what you were aspiring to anyway.

Think about it. Without that J-O-B you can now embark on something that inspires you. And competition makes you hungrier and more innovative. And an old flame, now extinguished, could open the door for the person really meant for you.

In short, stuff happens but it might not be that bad after all.

-54-
Bad Luck? Good Luck? Who Knows?

One day, a farmer had a wild stallion run off. His neighbors remarked, "Oh, what bad luck!" The farmer responded, "Bad luck? Good luck? Who knows?"

Later the stallion returned with a herd of wild horses. The neighbors remarked, "Wow, what good luck!" The farmer responded, "Bad luck? Good luck? Who knows?"

A day later the farmer's son broke his leg as he was thrown from a horse. His neighbors remarked, "Oh what bad luck!" The farmer responded, "Bad luck? Good luck? Who knows?"

A week later, the army came by to enlist all able-bodied young men for war. When they saw the boy's broken leg, they moved on ... and the army moved on to a battle that no one survived.

Events in your life don't stand on their own. They are each just scenes in a lifelong movie. And with each remember, "Bad luck? Good luck? Who knows?"

-55-
Seeking Conversation

Why do you go to networking events? There are probably lots of potential reasons. And those reasons change from event to event and from one time to another.

One reason you don't go to networking events, however, is to stand by your lonesome and quietly sip your coffee or whatever. Of course not.! You're there to engage in conversation.

This begs the question: How do you seek out people to talk to at events?

Know this: It is much easier to engage one person in conversation than a whole group.

So, when you arrive at an event or whenever you find yourself without someone to talk to, look for that person standing alone.

You know what? Chances are, that person is hoping for someone just like you to engage them in conversation. So, at next networking event, look for that person and go make a friend.

-56-
Be the Resource

Would you like to be known as a generous connector? Of course, you would.

Would you like to be considered a source of information and opportunities? That'd be great too.

How do you make this happen? It's simple.

Tell everyone you know that if they need anything ... anything at all ... to let you know. Clients. Information. Staff. Vendors. Whatever.

Tell them that you have a vast and growing network. And, while you cannot guarantee it can help them, let them know you would like to try.

And whether or not you're able to succeed, this will give you an opportunity to tap into your network and find ways to help others.

From this, in time, you will get the reputation of being a wonderful resource. And this is something that will serve to attract people to want to connect with you, thereby growing your network.

-57-
The Poison of Resentment

In 1994, a member of the media asked the newly elected president of South Africa, Nelson Mandela, if he'd hold a grudge against those who were responsible for his decades of wrongful imprisonment.

Mandela calmly replied "NO," and then continued with:

"Resentment is like drinking poison and then hoping it will kill your enemies."

While you might not have been wrongfully incarcerated for the better part of your adult life, no doubt you've been wronged somewhere along the way. In school. In your community. In your career. Whatever it was, let it go.

Holding on to anger won't change the past. Hoping for bad karma will never fix how you might have been wronged. The only true way forward is to forgive. Plus, moving on will allow you to free up energies and head space for more productive pursuits.

-58-
Don't Act Desperate

People want to be associated with helping you succeed. They really do. However, they do not want the responsibility of ensuring whether or not you survive professionally.

Think about it. If you act as if every networking relationship will make or break you, you'll likely have a lonely networking existence.

Remember, building great relationships is a powerful means of advancing a professional career or business. These connections can lead you to other great people, enlighten you with invaluable information, and open your life to wonderful opportunities.

This, however, is not a magic elixir. Great relationships don't happen overnight. And even once you have them, you can't expect that they'll come through for you on command.

So, if you need to close a deal at the last minute to hit a sales quota or require 11th hour heroics to get that promotion, don't expect networking to help.

-59-
In The Face of Tradition

Three women - Jessica Stubitsch, Morgan Van Lanen, and Erin DiMeglio - have one thing in common; they were each passionate about the sport they played and, as a result, they did not allow social norms to stand in their way.

Stubitsch played hockey at Northern Illinois University as a goalie for the men's team.

Van Lanen was a member of the Bark River-Harris High School wrestling team.

DiMeglio was a third-string quarterback for the South Plantation High School.

Despite what might be the conventional wisdom that proclaims that "girls can't play hockey, wrestle or play football" these three were undeterred.

But social norms don't stop with sports. They are all around just waiting for you to defy them. Don't allow the mindsets of yesterday to dictate your future.

Rather, follow your heart and passionately do what you want to do.

-60-
Don't Foul Up the Follow Up

Networking events are wonderful. They really are. The conversations can be exhilarating. And the whole experience productive.

But you risk squandering the whole experience if you fail to follow up or follow through.

Networking is not just idle conversation. Embedded in those conversations are vows and commitments. If you pledged to reconnect, do so. If you offered to introduce them, make it happen. If you indicated you would send them something, get it sent.

Know this, very few people follow through on what they say they are going to do. That's a sad, but true reality.

Given that, if you are committed to following up and following through, you immediately elevate yourself above a significant portion of the networking population.

So, don't foul up your follow up. Do what you say you're going to do.

-61-
The Cloak of Invincibility

Everyone knows that feeling of apprehension you get when walking into a room with lots of people and only a few you know relatively well.

Your breathing quickens. Your muscles tense. You can feel sweat starting to build.

While there is no comfort in knowing this is perfectly natural, take comfort in knowing you can ease this tension. Here's how:

As you enter, remind yourself that networking is about helping others and you are there to do just that. After all, you are there to share a plethora of experience and a vast network.

As such, this mindset gives you a cloak of invincibility. It transforms you from being a stranger that the room may judge and potentially reject into someone there to perform a heroic act. Afterall, through your network you have the power to make someone's day, if not completely change their world. And everyone will welcome that.

-62-
Attention: Important Meeting

Sound advice for successful networking is to treat each and every encounter with others as if it were an important business meeting. Why? Because it is.

Any person you have the chance to interact with has tremendous potential. Each and every one is a gateway to other useful contacts. They are the key – whether direct or indirect – to lots of referrals. And they are conduits to information sources that can take you to new heights.

While they may never say it (or even know it), these people believe that you will treat their contacts, referrals and information sources the same way you treat them.

So, do yourself a huge favor; treat everyone with kindness and respect. Be attentive when others speak. And make them feel as if they matter. Because they really do.

-63-
Nothing Fails Like Success

Repeat championships in major sports tends to be the exception rather than the rule. Certainly, there are many reasons for this. Chief among them is that following a championship season it's hard to push to maintain the same drive and work ethic.

In short, a sense of complacency infects everyone. It's not uncommon, in fact, that defending champions don't make the playoffs.

This is not limited to sports, however. Noble prize winners seldom even come close to matching their award-winning achievement. And in corporate America, a Wall Street darling might not hold that position for long.

Nothing herein suggests that you should avoid achievement. By all means, have goals and aspirations, then drive hard to see them through.

As you do, though, you should guard against complacency. Continue to do the things that got you where you are and commit to staying at that level.

-64-
Do You Just Belong?

A great way of connecting with a passionate, diverse core of people is to become part of groups or organizations that interest you. To be effective, however, this should not be a loose affiliation but rather an active involvement.

After all, a productive network is built on mutual knowing, liking and trusting, and "just belonging" won't make that happen.

While there are no definite rules regarding the appropriate level of involvement, there is a simple test.

Ask yourself this, regarding any organization to which we belong: "If I weren't at a meeting or event, would I be missed?"

If you answer no, you simply need to become more involved.

If, however, your answer is yes, I'd be missed, you're doing great. You're not merely a name on a roster, but a face, a handshake, and a smile that people can know, like and trust.

-65-
Networking And Social Media

While there was a day that some proclaimed the Internet as just a fad, others re-tooled it. They took a novel approach and made it so that we could all not just see it but contribute to it too.

We know this as social media, and it has completely shifted how you can discover and share news, information and other content.

Certainly, social media gets a bad rap as an expansive online rumor mill or coffee club. If you approach it correctly, however, it can be a valuable networking tool for connecting and communicating with others. While you should not spend countless hours reading idle chit-chat from others, you should make time each day to learning from others and contributing to them as well.

No, the Internet is not a passing fad. But you just might be if you don't learn to utilize its potential.

-66-
The House of 1,000 Mirrors

In a far-away village, there was the House of 1,000 Mirrors. It was a magical place with dozens upon dozens of reflective glasses of all shapes and sizes.

One day, a happy dog ventured in, eagerly bounding through the doorway ... ears lifted high and tail wagging quickly. The dog delighted in finding 1,000 other happy little dogs looking back.

"WOW! What a wonderful place. I will come back often," the smiling dog thought.

A short time later, a suspicious little dog slowly entered ... head and tail hanging low. To his shock, this dog saw staring back 1,000 unfriendly dogs. Completely panicked, this dog scampered out, vowing never to go back."

Do you know what? You visit the House of 1,000 Mirrors every day. All the faces in the world reflect exactly what you project.

So, what kind of reflections do you want to see?

-67-
Successful People Have Goals

Successful people have goals. They have goals for lots of things. Networking activity. Prospecting efforts. Sales made. Referrals made and received. And much, much more.

Successful people have goals. They write them down. They share their goals with others. They review them often.

Successful people have goals. Goals that, from time to time, they fail to hit. And they're okay with that. Why? Because successful people tend to set goals that stretch them and make them work. As a result, they risk failing.

But successful people know that falling short of a goal is no great sin. They realize that the real potential mistake is setting their goals too low. Why?

Because successful people understand that with easily attainable goals, they may always hit their mark. But by always hitting their mark they are, in essence, leaving money on the table.

-68-
Don't Sell

Networking is about establishing and building relationships. It's not really about prospecting or selling.

In fact, those who attempt to do business within their network before it's appropriate, end up with counterproductive results.

The reality is that people love to buy things they perceive will help them. What they don't love, however, is feeling like they are being sold.

This is not to suggest that you never do business with those in your network. On the contrary, you can ... and should. This will likely be your best client base, as well as a great source of referrals.

What this does suggest is not being too hasty promoting business within your network. Take your time with it. Let them come to know, like and trust you. Once that happens, chances are they will want to buy from you. And then you'll really never have to sell to them.

-69-
Explore Their Passion

Without a doubt, networking events and other opportunities to engage people in conversation are great ways to build relationships. At times, however, the conversation can become a little trite. Same questions. Rehearsed answers. It can feel like Charlie Brown's teacher talking. You know: Wah, Wah, Wah.

To break up the monotony, take some advice from American psychologist and self-help author, Susan Jeffers. In her book *Dare To Connect* she suggests that instead of the customary question, "What do you do?" consider asking, "What do you LOVE to do?"

Jeffers goes on to share that this twist on a traditional question "offers a better picture of the inside of the person instead of their outer role." Plus, there is an added bonus, as the answer to this question will contain more raw material for keeping the conversation alive as well as fun.

-70-
Express Quiet Confidence

People love passion. They love enthusiasm. They are drawn to it. They feed off it. It actually inspires them to become a better version of themselves.

Therefore, a great way to help build your network is to carry yourself in a manner that exudes enthusiasm as to who you are, what you do, as well as what you stand for.

This, however, doesn't mean to demonstrate this passion you have to be loud, animated, excited, or gregarious. In fact, in extremes these attributes can be off-putting and detrimental. But even at reasonable levels these characteristics are unnecessarily.

Rather enthusiasm and passion are best conveyed by how you carry yourself. You need only exhibit a confidence and optimistic demeanor that subtly whispers, "I believe in who I am and what I can do." If you consistently do this, your passion and enthusiasm will come through loud and clear.

-71-
The Subsequent Steps

Let's be honest. There is no shortage of ideas. They are simply easy to come by. They happen in the shower. And they'll hit you while you're mowing the lawn, vacuuming the house, and commuting in traffic. Ideas are downright easy.

What's hard is getting started. The first few words of your book idea can be a chore. Making the first pitch on that new initiative you've concocted is frightening. The first step of any journey can seem daunting.

Yes, the first step is the hardest part. But the most important steps are all the ones that come after the that. The first one gets you moving, but the ones after that create momentum. And it's this momentum that helps you see things through.

In fact, without these subsequent steps, your effort on the hardest part is wasted.

So, to achieve on any idea, get started and keep stepping.

-72-
Know The Three P's

In developing your professional relationships, over time you need to create a mutual sense of "knowing."

This, however, cannot be limited to others only knowing who you are and what you do. And, likewise, you need to know more than just these things about the other person.

This "knowing" must encompass all aspects of the three P's:

The first "P" is, Past Information: Where they are from? Where they went to school?

The second "P" is Personal Lives: What is their marital status? Do they children? What hobbies or interests do they have?

The final "P" is Professional Background: What did they study? What degrees and licenses do they have? Who have they worked for? What are the unique experiences or specialties that they have?

It is upon this "knowing" that the entire relationship is built, so it's best you invest some time into it.

-73-
Finish Things

Leaving high school before completing leaves you short of a diploma. Dropping out of the marathon at mile 22 leaves you with designation of "Did Not Finish." Getting a bathroom remodel 90 percent complete leaves you only with an angry spouse.

In life, it's not a matter of what you start. Rather, you'll be judged by what you finish.

Yes, it's great to have many proverbial "irons in the fire" and it's good to be diversified by having lots of things underway. But it's equally important to see things through. In short, there's tremendous value in bringing things to completion.

So, from time to time ask yourself, "Am I just busy doing things or am I focused on getting things done?"

Remember to take the time to knock things off your list and not just add things to it.

-74-
Ask To Assist

Networking is about giving – doing things for people around you. From this, people want to know you. Chances are, they can't help but come to like you. And, with these two things, their trust in you will grow. In short, through helping others your relationship builds.

To this end, look for ways to help your network. To empower this, make it a habit of inquiring of your network how you can assist them. Probe with questions, like:

"Who would you like to meet?"
"What opportunities are you looking for?"
"What are some challenges you currently face?"

Or

"How can I assist you in meeting your goals?"

If you consistently do this, in time, you'll find that others will be attracted to you. But they won't just be interested in getting from you; they will also be interested in helping you too.

-75-
Four Eighteen

In 2002, Principia College receiver Lewis Howes had a reasonable goal for each game: Accumulate at least 100 receiving yards. And with hard work and determination, he achieved this goal in every game.

During one game, however, Howes hit his goal in the first quarter. His team needed it, though. Principia was in a "dog fight" against rival Martin Luther College.

So, Lewis kept going. To keep pace with their opponent, he accumulated another 100 yards. And then another 100. And then 100 yards one more time. When the dust had settled on the game, Lewis Howes had recorded a total of 418 yards, which was an NCAA record in all division for years and years.

The lesson is this: Set worthwhile goals and work hard to achieve them. And once you do, keep going. Chances are someone out there needs you to.

-76-
Become a Copycat

Do you want to become better at networking? Sure, you do. Everyone wants to become more proficient at connecting with others and building productive relationships in their life. From these relationships come other great contacts, referrals, information, opportunities, and the list goes on.

Now, if you're at a loss as to how you can become better at networking, here's a surefire means of learning:

Find someone who is already successful and figure out what they do. After all, successful people got where they are via building productive relationships. And they likely have networking insights that will push you up the learning curve.

Ask for a few minutes of their time so you can inquire as to how they build relationships.

And when you see them in public or at events, observe them. Watch how they interact.

The bottom line is this: Don't reinvent the wheel, rather copy someone else's.

-77-
30,000 People Can't Be Wrong

In 2003, a group of researchers embarked on an ambitious, multi-year study involving over 30,000 households across the United States.

Among the many things that this team was trying to determine was what impact additional income had on people's generosity. What the researchers were able to determine was that for every additional dollar of income, household contributed on average 14 more cents. That's no big revelation, right?

Remember, however, this study spanned multiple years. So, the researchers were also able to look at the impact that generosity had on household income. What they found was stunning. For every dollar of additional contribution, household earnings grew on average a whopping $3.74.

What the researchers clearly showed is that being generous, while serving to help others, will somehow help you too. Knowing this, the question shouldn't be should I be helping others. But rather how can I help others.

-78-
Don't Monopolize

There is no doubt that you're interesting. How you came to this place in life is likely intriguing. Your personal life is full of engaging stories. You're a tremendous reservoir of useful information and insightful opinions. And there is much you can say about what you do and how you do it.

That said, as interesting as you certainly are, you aren't so interesting that what you have to say should consume the entire subject matter of a conversation. After all, no one is that interesting.

When you get into conversations with others, don't just talk about yourself. Keep it interesting. Talk about you, talk about them and talk about others.

At the very worst, you should have an equal split between what you say and what you hear. Because, ironically, the more you talk about you, the less you appear to have to offer.

-79-
It's Just a Patch

Setbacks are part of life, right? Some are big, some are small and a good many are in between.

- You'll have relationships that go sideways.
- Your best laid plans simply won't work out.
- That promotion won't come through.
- A raise will be smaller than expected.
- A great opportunity will just disappear.
- A client will refuse to pay an invoice.
- A vendor will hit you with a larger than expected bill.
- The water heater will fail.
- Your car won't start.

And at times, it feels like all of this is hitting at once and the whole darn world is conspiring against you. It's easy to get down. Don't.

Take a moment to gather yourself. Remind yourself that setbacks happen. Keep working hard. Stay optimistic. This is not your new place in life. This is merely a patch you need to work through.

-80-
NetworkWise

Speaker, super-connector, and social architect Adam Connors has coined a term ... NetworkWise.

What does it mean? Adam will tell you that it's a verb that means "taking a proactive approach to relationship development with the ultimate goal of benefiting another individual."

And he will elaborate by explaining that the term NetworkWise is about "establishing value by always welcoming the opportunity to collaborate through conversation, as well as cultivating a mindset that is immersed in learning the science and art of networking."

He will further share that NetworkWise is about viewing networking "as a habit and skill that needs to be exercised or it will atrophy."

And finally, Adam Connors will summarize that NetworkWise is about continually interacting with and benefitting those around you and not just when you might need something. This is the best way to establish essential connections, gain influence and create overall personal fulfillment.

-81-
Everyone Has a Plan Until

In preparing for an upcoming fight, legendary heavyweight boxer Mike Tyson was asked what he thought of the strategy his challenger was boasting about. Without much elaboration, the defending champion responded, "Everyone has a plan until he gets punched in the face."

In short, Tyson was reminding everyone that no matter how much his opponents plotted and schemed, he would have a say as to how the strategy was to unfold.

And he is right, both inside and outside the boxing ring.

Yes, strategizing is imperative. All successful people do it. But successful people know that strategies are formed in a vacuum. And once exposed to outside forces or unforeseen circumstances, every strategy is put to the test.

So, beyond the initial strategy, successful people contemplate contingencies. Because no matter how much effort goes into a strategy, they may just need those contingencies when reality steps forward and punches it in the face.

-82-
The Strength of Weak Ties

If you're like most people, you tend to gravitate towards those you know very well. It's natural. It's comfortable. It just seems right.

However, if you are looking for real networking potential, consider the person you hardly know at all. Think about it.

While the people you know well generally think like you and have similar interests, you also have a tremendous overlap in contacts. They know many of the same people as you and the potential to meet someone new through them is low.

But when the connection is weak and you don't know the person well, there is little overlap between your respective contacts. Thus, the potential to grow your networking contacts is enormous.

While there is tremendous comfort in being with those you know well, there is enormous potential and strength with the weak ties in your life.

-83-
A Thing Called Guts!

American author Louis Adamic wrote in his 1944 essay *A Study In Courage* …

"There is a certain blend of courage, integrity, character, and principle which has no satisfactory dictionary name, but has been called different things at different times in different countries. Our American name for it is "guts.""

America has been called "The Land of Opportunity." While that is arguably still true, opportunity in and of itself is not enough.

To see opportunity through takes a strong character, one that can create a bold vision that others can clearly see and contribute to. It requires establishing principles that guide individual efforts and interaction with others.

It needs a commitment to integrity, so the right things are done especially when others aren't doing them. To see opportunity through necessitates the courage to work tirelessly even when a successful outcome is not clear.

No, opportunity alone is not enough. To see it through takes guts.

-84-
Giving Never Gets Old

The joy you get from helping others never really fades.

In a study, researchers gave approximately 100 participants five dollars per day for five days. Randomly, half the participants were instructed to spend the windfall on themselves, each day purchasing the same thing, like a great cup of coffee or a snack.

The other half were instructed to use their daily money to benefit another in a consistent fashion, like a leaving an extraordinarily tip or a donation.

Throughout the process, the researchers measured the level of happiness the participants felt relative to their daily habit of spending or giving. While the happiness of the spenders dropped as the experiment wore on, the happiness of the givers held firm.

Helping others is a joyful thing, for you and the person you're helping. And it's good to know that as you endeavor to help those around you, that joyful feeling will never really get old.

-85-
Stars & Stripes Forever

In 1776, a young woman was officially "read out" of the Quaker community for marrying outside of her faith. You see, she had fallen in love with and married an Episcopalian named John Ross.

Literally overnight, she was cut off from the life she had known. Despite this setback, John and Betsy began a life together. He served in the army. She started a sewing business. Together they attended church.

John introduced her to Christ Church, which included as parishioners Benjamin Franklin and five others who would eventually sign the Declaration of Independence, as well as George Washington.

At about that same time, George Washington came to the belief that for the revolutionary effort to be successful in rebelling against the King of England, the American troops needed a single flag to unify the 13 colonies. To sew that flag, he did not have to look far.

And, yes, networking played a role in this nation's Independence.

-86-
Nix the Quid Pro Quo

Do you operate in a quid pro quo world? You know, one where your every move is measured against a potential outcome?

One where what you do or don't do is contingent on others acting first or promising to act shortly thereafter? If so, stop.

Trying to match your actions and efforts with likely outcomes is a losing proposition. You'll pass on wonderful opportunities because "what's in it for you" might not be readily apparent. You'll burn significant time and energy sizing up situations to ensure you get your due.

Quid pro quo is for corporate dealmakers, financiers, and pro sports teams who endeavor to match value tit for tat.

It, however, is not well suited at all for building relationships. It has no place in a world where you simply have to trust that your efforts will come back to you.

If you have a quid pro quo mindset, nix it.

-87-
Embrace Chaos

In October 2014, workers within the London Underground staged a walkout. This sent thousands upon thousands of commuters into utter chaos trying to find alternate ways to get to work. Fortunately, the strike only lasted 48 hours and quickly things got back to normal, and the chaos subsided.

Interestingly, however, research determined that about five percent of the commuting population did not revert to their pre-strike commuting habits. It seems that the strike had upended their normal routine and, in so doing, they found a better routine.

We humans are creatures of habit, fixated on patterns. And while these patterns create efficiencies in our lives, they also stifle creativity and critical thinking.

Chaos might disrupt the efficiencies we enjoy, but it also forces us to re-examine our lives. It provides us an opportunity to look for new solutions. In inspires us to create and invent. So, while chaos is never fun, the learning opportunities it might create is reason enough for us to embrace it.

-88-
Interest in Others Equals Interest in You

No doubt, you have an interest in getting to know those who have an interest in you. Right? It's simply human nature.

Knowing this, you should make this notion work in your favor. To do so, acknowledge those around you. Make eye contact. Smile. Say hello.

You see, when you acknowledge those around you, they'll want to get to know you that much more.

When you acknowledge those around you, you make them feel important and from this they cannot help but like you.

And when you acknowledge others, they become more comfortable around you and, in the process, become more trusting.

So, make it a habit to greet everyone you encounter with eye contact, a smile, and a friendly hello. From this, they'll perceive you as being outgoing and friendly, which is just the type that everyone wants in their network.

-89-
Have You Met?

A linchpin to building a successful network is adding value to others. By adding value, people want to know you and become almost compelled to like and trust you. Once you surrender to this notion that adding value is key to building a network, you need to set about finding ways to do that.

That said, there are many ways in which you can you can add value to others. You can make referrals. You can share information. You can simply encourage or celebrate others.

The most lasting way to add value, however, is by bringing people together from different segments of your life. You see, when you connect two people, you set in motion a networking multiplier, because those new contacts share information, referrals, opportunities, and (YES) more contacts.

So, if you want to add lasting, network-building value to someone, connect them to someone they don't know.

-90-
Say It with A Smile

The most powerful thing you have to offer the world is simply your smile. It's true.

Your smile can light up a darkened mood. It can lift a heavy heart. It has the energy to move an entire room. It really can! You can do so much good with your smile. Nothing else about you has this power.

Knowing this, be sure to meet any and every connection with a smile. As you approach someone, it's your smile upon which they will fixate. When talking to someone on the phone, believe it or not, they can hear your smile. When you send an e-mail, somehow your smiling demeanor comes through too.

So, make smiling a habit. This is the best way to ensure that your initial contacts become lasting relationships.

-91-
Tomorrow is Never Promised

Domenic Romanelli, boys' soccer coach for the seven-time state champion St. Francis DeSales high school, drills this notion into his players: "Tomorrow is Never Promised."

He encourages them to set lofty goals and work hard to achieve them. But then he reminds them that no matter what, nothing is for sure.

They might be better prepared, but a bad stretch could turn the whole game.

They might have the better team, but a fluke goal could end the season.

They might be incredibly fit and yet an unfortunate misstep could end a career.

Tomorrow is never promised. But this mantra is not limited to the soccer pitch.

In life, there are no guarantees either. Have hopes, dreams and aspirations and work tirelessly to achieve them. However, always remember that sometimes fate has its own plan and that there is always the potential for outside forces to intervene. Tomorrow is never promised.

-92-
Use the F Word

You aren't perfect. And neither are the people around you. As such, it's only a matter of time before someone, somehow creates hardship for you. Some will be big, other small and many transgressions lay somewhere in between.

Whatever the case, in these moments what do you do? Simple. You're best to quickly use the F-word. No, not that F-word. The appropriate F-word is forgiveness. Take hold of your emotions and quietly allow any malice or resentment built inside you to quietly subside.

No, this is not easy. In fact, it can at times be hard. But when you forgive, you can move forward without a lingering grudge zapping your energy or distracting your focus.

Plus, this is a great way to build trust within your network. You see, when you forgive, people become comfortable dealing with you. They know that you will eventually look past their occasional errors and shortcomings.

Use the F word.

-93-
The Power of Praise

According to David Dunn, author of *Try Giving Yourself Away*, "The person who praises another enriches themselves far more than the one praised. To praise is an investment in happiness."

This is so true. You see, whenever you praise another (whether publicly or privately ... whether formally or informally) you share a little bit of yourself. After all, you've taken the time to notice someone's efforts and then more time to make a point of recognizing them.

And, yes, people appreciate being recognized for the value they bring to the world. Whether it's a job well done, an act of kindness or whatever, when you take the time to praise someone, the joy you provide them seems to grow and radiate back over to you. It's like a wonderful, but mysterious, quirk of nature.

You don't need to fully understand this works. Knowing it works is enough. With this insight, go find someone and praise them.

-94-
Houston ... We Have a Problem

"Houston ... We have a problem." In April 1970, James Lovell uttered these words following an explosion aboard Apollo 13.

His journey to the surface of the moon was over. His life was literally on the line.
What lay ahead was nothing but adversity and uncertainty.

But in that moment, Lovell wanted to know if his shipmates were content with letting fate determine their destiny or whether they were committed to controlling the course of their lives. So, he asked them "Gentleman, what are your intentions?"

The crew of Apollo 13 responded. Using ingenuity, they guided the crippled Apollo 13 successfully back to Mother Earth.

While your situation may never be anywhere near as dire as that of Apollo 13, you will face adversity. In these moments, *What Are Your Intentions?*

Just as with the crew of Apollo 13, commit to control the course of your life. If you do this, no matter your situation, there is no doubt that you will have a safe landing.

-95-
The Place for Humor

"There is no place for humor in business." If you've heard this, don't buy into it.

Think about it. This attitude serves to strip a degree of enjoyment out of what amounts to the lion's share of your day.

Yes, some humor is simply not in good taste. Avoid that. But that doesn't mean you need to abandon humor altogether, right?

Useful humor need be nothing more than a clever comment about the weather, a local sports team or the quality of office coffee. And any of these will ease the general tension of a professional environment.

Remember, humor reminds others that you're human. It is something with which anyone can identify. Plus, it's nearly impossible to dislike someone who has made them laugh or is genuinely laughing at something funny.

So, don't be afraid to yuk it up in business.

-96-
Would You Stop?

In his book, *No One Gets There Alone*, author Dr. Rob Bell poses an insightful question: "Would you stop?"

To elaborate, after a grueling one-mile, open-water swim, Bell was 32 miles into the biking portion of a triathlon when his back tire blew out. With neither the equipment nor ability to affect a repair, his race seemed to be over.

Then two competitors stopped, sacrificing their standing in the race, and helped Bell back into the competition. As he raced on, he couldn't help but ponder, "Would I have stopped?"

That was a moment of great inspiration for him. Bell now not only stops when he sees someone in need, he actively looks for the opportunity. And he doesn't limit this to athletic competition. It has become a way of life, making small sacrifices to aid others.

So, when he asks others "Would you stop?", it's not really a question, but rather an invitation to be part of his team of selfless heroes.

-97-
A Million Dollars Is Hanging in The Balance

How would you conduct yourself if a million dollars were hanging in the balance? In other words, if you knew that a contact or business encounter would lead to a seven-figure payday, how would you act? What would you say? Who would you be?

You'd certainly be professional and on time. You would be attentive, courteous, and reverent. In short, you'd put forth the very best version of yourself.

Guess what? In every moment of every day and with every encounter, a million dollars is hanging in the balance. It's true. That meeting with the new client? Absolutely. The vendor making a delivery? You bet. That "cold" call that interrupts your day? Yep!

You see, with every encounter you're dealing with at least one other. And that "one other" knows countless more. Over time, this builds to a very real potential of a seven-figure payday. So, act accordingly. A million dollars is hanging in the balance.

-98-
Don't Pry

The start of any relationship begins with getting to know someone. This process involves a completely un-orchestrated volley of asking questions, listening, and asking more questions.

Although this is important to developing solid networking relationships, you should not endeavor to get any more information than they are willing to give. The extent to which others let themselves be known is personal to them. Some things they freely share. On other things, they are a tad more guarded. Respect those boundaries. Don't press. Don't pry.

Yes, great relationships involve showing that you're interested in knowing others. But great relationships also involve others liking and trusting you. So, when you sense you've overstepped your bounds, back off and casually take your inquiry in another direction.

When you do, you'll continue to learn about them and at the same time quietly build the extent to which they like and trust you.

-99-
In Search of Likability

Of one thing you can be sure, everyone wants to be liked. It's an innate desire that's as old as recorded time.

Moreover, people want to associate with those who like them. In fact, they want to surround themselves with those that simply delight in who they are and to achieve that they subconsciously return the feeling. So, here's the lesson: If you want to build your network far and wide with people who like you, make a point of finding ways to like others.

With everyone you encounter, take a quick survey of their interpersonal characteristics. While they may not be perfect (as none of us are), no doubt there is something about them that makes you declare "I like this person."

Whatever it is, seize upon that one thing and focus on it. Your affection for them will grow and that will come through as you interact. And then, they will grow to like you in return.

-100-
Shoeless Ron Hunter

In 2008, Ron Hunter, then basketball coach at Indiana University-Purdue University of Indianapolis, began coaching shoeless. He did so not because he could not afford shoes. He did so because he could not pass up helping those in need.

You see, Hunter was looking to draw attention to fact that millions and millions of children around the world go barefoot because they don't have access to shoes ... and even if they did, they could not afford them.

Through this awareness, Hunter inspired others to coach shoeless. And through this combined influence, they created a movement that resulted in supporters and fans donating thousands and thousands of shoes for international charities.

No matter who you are, no matter what you do, you have influence. Do your corner of the world a favor: No matter how big or small, use your influence for good.

-101-
Mistakes Are Part of Life

In her book *Respond with Confidence*, body language trainer Nancy Ganzekaufer indicates that everybody makes mistakes, but not everyone effectively deals with them. She shares, "It is common for mistakes to cause you to "get stuck." Rather than moving past the mistake, you replay the scenario over and over in your mind, wishing you had done something differently."

Ganzekaufer then reminds you that ruminating over the situation doesn't fix it. It just becomes an exhausting waste of time and energy. Her advice for moving forward is to first admit the mistake to yourself and the others you've harmed. And it's always important to make a heartfelt apology as a part of this.

Beyond this, focus on rectifying the situation. What was the origin of your mistake? And how can you both fix it and avoid it in the future? Remember, mistakes are part of life. Growing from them should be too.

There you have it—101 essays. But we wanted to offer a bonus essay. Before we do, if you're interested in exploring other books, content, and programs by Frank Agin, visit frankagin.com or simply search "Frank Agin" on whatever platform you use to get great content.

-102-
Mining For Results

Tim Shurr, corporate trainer, motivational speaker, and high-performance psychologist, shared in his book *The Power of Optimism: Attitude Training for Those Who Want More from Life*:

"Be persistent. You never know when that next step will produce the results you've been looking for. Don't make the same mistake the miner made when he stopped digging just six inches short of gold."

As Shurr will tell you, life is not easy. Actually, it's hard. You will have setbacks. You will have bad days ... or even weeks. And even when you experience good times, they'll be sprinkled with challenging things.

Despite that, always keep a laser-focus on the things that you want in life. And whatever you need to be to get there, put those activities on the top of your daily to-do list. Hoping that achievement finds you never works.

Rather, what does is mining away with persistent action. Day after day, no matter what.

About The Author

Frank Agin is president of AmSpirit Business Connections, which empowers entrepreneurs, sales representatives, and professionals to become successful and gain more referrals through networking.

He also shares information and insights on professional relationships, business networking and best practices for generating referrals on his Networking Rx podcast and through various professional programs.

Finally, Frank is the author of several books, including *Foundational Networking: Building Know, Like & Trust to Create a Life of Extraordinary Success*. See all his books and programs at frankagin.com. You can reach him at frankagin@amspirit.com.

www.ingramcontent.com/pod-product-compliance
Lightning Source LLC
Chambersburg PA
CBHW040757220326

41597CB00029BB/4972